BawB's Raven Feathers
Reflections on the simple things in life

VOLUME IV

Robert Chomany

INVERMERE PRESS • CALGARY, CANADA

Copyright © 2014, Robert Chomany

All rights reserved. No part of this publication may be reproduced or transmitted in any form or by any means, electronic or mechanical, including photocopying, recording, or any information storage and retrieval system without permission in writing from the author.

ISBN 978-0-9918821-8-2 (v. 4 : softcover)

Illustration: Jessee Wise
Book Design: Fiona Raven Book Design
Chief Editor: Rachel Small, Faultless Finish Editing
Proofreader: Carrie Mumford

Published by
Robert Chomany
Calgary, Alberta, Canada
bchomany@telusplanet.net

Printed in the United States of America

www.bawbsravenfeathers.net

This series of books is dedicated to my mom—without her love, patience and guidance I would not be the man I am today. She taught me to appreciate compassion, to stand alone, and to be proud of who I am, and she gave me strength to pursue my dreams.

Not just words do I share with you, I send a smile each day.
I send it in the wind for you, to help in some small way.

Confidence

It goes without saying that your confidence is probably not always as strong as you would like it to be. It can sometimes be shadowed by doubt, which, if left unchallenged, can evolve into insecurities. There is no cause for alarm if you lack confidence in your ability to do something, as sometimes it is healthy fear that causes you to hesitate or stand down entirely from a challenge. But this healthy fear might just be a precursor to some absolute adrenaline-pumping thrills. If this is the case, work through the fear and have some fun.

Most of us have been in situations where we would have felt better if we had known more, and this lack of knowledge played on our level of confidence. Perhaps you're hesitant about performing an action in front of a group of people—public speaking, for example. Speaking on a subject requires you to be well versed in that topic: you may need to do some research. But learning about something you're interested in will not only increase your knowledge base, but also your ability to speak on that subject. Once you are more comfortable with something, your confidence builds, and the learning becomes a welcomed experience.

Should you ever find yourself in a room surrounded by new and interesting people, always keep in mind that you have no idea how much everyone in the room knows. Perhaps most know even less than you do about a conversation topic at hand—so remember this, and use it to your advantage. Take the time to stay up to date on the things you're interested in, and you will naturally become more confident in the knowledge of them. What follows is practicing what you have learned, which then becomes experience, which builds confidence . . . you get the idea.

Without confidence, you may wonder if you are good enough, strong enough, or capable enough to accomplish a task. Well, with practice, you won't only become good at something, you will become the best at it, and this achievement will instill confidence for the next task you take on. By climbing one day at a time, one can ascend the tallest of mountains. Set yourself up for success by learning as you go and by remembering each step you took along the way when you get to the top. Become confident in being who you are by believing that you can take on any challenge and learn from it, succeed at it, and move on to the next. Live your life one day at a time, live for each moment, and be confident that the next moment will be that much better than the last.

You should feel proud to speak out loud
if there's something you need to say.
Just stand up tall and give it your all,
and believe in yourself today.

You have the power to just be you
and stand out amongst the crowd.
Lift your spirits to where they belong
and let yourself be proud.

Remember those times
when you heard yourself say,
"I should have made a stand"?
Well it's time you stopped feeding
those birds in the bush
and held a few in your hand.

Don't hide those things
that the world needs to know,
like that something you're good at
but are too scared to show.

Don't be afraid to stand up straight
and let your energy loom;
just be yourself and wear a smile
and soon you'll own the room.

If you can't see the horizon each day,
then your head is not held high.
You should be seeing the morning sun—
point your smile towards the sky.

Do you ever think of everyone else
instead of thinking of you?
Do others get the credit first
for doing what it is you do?
Just for a change in your normal routine,
make today your day in the sun.
Believe in you and all that you are:
today you are number one.

Be proud of you and smile today,
show the world that you're fine;
just be you and happy too,
to live by your own design.

Explore the options that present themselves,
have a look at one or two.
Take a chance and have some fun,
find your courage and believe in you.

Don't be afraid to take that chance,
or put on something new.
No matter what happens you have to try
to feel better being you.

Do you care enough to really commit
to the challenges life throws your way?
Can you believe in yourself without hesitation
and stand behind what you say?
Walk your path with your head held high
and keep the horizon in sight;
if opportunity presents itself,
you'll need to know that it's right.

Believe in yourself and find your balance,
take a breath or two.
The only shadows you should ever see
are the shadows caused by you.
The light from your soul can be cast to the world
by simply being true,
and the inner confidence you'll then create
will show in all you do.

Doubt

In a book filled with positivity and inspiration, where does doubt fit in? Doubt is often a subconscious reaction, even in positive situations. Someone or something makes you smile, and then for just one brief second, you doubt that happiness you feel. Doubt makes you compete with yourself: part of you may, for a moment, doubt you can do something, and part of you knows you would love to try. In a balanced world of yin and yang, doubt is required to present or complement challenges, and to help us recognize them.

Doubt is something we seem to learn at a young age. I don't believe we are born with it. How on earth could we ever survive if we thought we didn't have the ability to do things as infants? Learning to talk, we simply mimicked the words and sounds we heard without doubting our ability to do so; learning to walk, we had no knowledge of gravity and therefore no doubt about what we were doing; riding a bike for the first time, we might have attempted the task with fear of the unknown but not with doubt in our abilities. We simply needed positive encouragement when we were young, and a little fear to keep us safe in our attempts to accomplish new things. Doubt started creeping into our lives when we started meeting more difficult challenges, perhaps through social pressure.

Maybe doubt entered your mind after an introduction to a dare at a young age. Someone in your group doubted you would or could do something and dared you to do it, and you either succeeded or failed. And if you failed, the experience probably left you with a shadow of a doubt that has followed you for as long as you can remember.

If it is truly a learned response, then we can unlearn it as well, and replace it with positive thoughts and aspirations. I think that as we get older, feelings of doubt more easily morph into hope, and then into other positive feelings. Perhaps it is safe to say that as we get more comfortable with who we are and our abilities, feelings of doubt sometimes become feelings of wonder. You might even start to wonder why you haven't done something before, rather than doubt you ever could.

When it comes to being you, there is no doubt you can achieve anything you put your mind to if you give it the effort it deserves.

A shadow of doubt is simply that:
a place where light doesn't shine.
Just by being confident
you can make that space divine.

That moment of time between each smile
is a moment you won't get back.
It's often a time to get caught up in thinking
about the things you lack.
Don't waste this time that's important to you—
believe in who you are.
Revisit the positive places you've been
and leave the door ajar.

Today be here enjoying life,
with every step you take,
choose to see the good in living,
and be happy for your own sake.
Take a minute to see the world
from the inside looking out,
and start this day with a positive smile
so there is no room for doubt.

How wonderful it is to greet the day with a clear and open mind;
each breath we take reminds us now to leave yesterday behind.

We always try to do what's right,

but what's right according to whom?

Is the right thing always right for the world,

or is it something that's right for you?

Believe in the things that you do for you,

because at the end of the day,

the path you're on you have chosen for you,

so you should be leading the way.

Trust in you to do the right thing.
Needing help just means you are learning.
Ask someone who's been there before,
to find knowledge for which you're yearning.

Challenge is good to hone your skills,
and timelines to keep you on track,
but if you don't ask those questions you have,
you'll soon be out of whack.

Have you ever wished for a little sign
that everything was right?
Have you ever been wakened by wondering things
in the middle of the night?
The signs will come if you can relax
and look at things much clearer;
let go of those pesky feelings of doubt
and smile at you in the mirror.

Have you ever wondered why
you pondered a thought,
and was the thinking you did
worth the outcome you got?
If all along you really believed,
yet planted a small seed of doubt,
was it worth it then to question your thinking,
and allow the seed to sprout?

If there's ever an ounce of doubt in your mind,
then your mind's not in the right place;
positive thinking and belief in yourself
will bring a smile back to your face.

Do you ever doubt or question
the you who lives inside?
Have you ever had the feeling
that you ought to run and hide?
Life is based on choices,
with options and direction,
so learn to trust your inner voice
and listen to your reflection.

Work at simply being yourself,
practicing all you've been taught,
then one day you'll simply find
that you're happy with all you've got.
On that day you'll know for sure
that what you've done is right;
your energy will be felt by all
as you shine your brightest light.

Success

Does success come easy to you? Or do you know someone who never seems to fail, someone who is always successful? Success is nothing more than a state of mind. If your belief in yourself is strong, then you will find success in all your failures, because failing will mean you tried and are learning what is required to succeed. If you simply smile for no reason, then you will succeed at being happy for that moment.

We can find great delight in our successes. They are things we can share, things we can feel, and things we can hold up as achievements. But success isn't winning or losing; success isn't being better than; success is simply a means of recognizing fulfillment. Success shouldn't be measured in any way—it should simply be enjoyed. I don't think it's possible to be more or less successful than anyone else, as success means something different for each of us. It could be something as simple as successfully baking a pie, or something as complex as walking on the moon.

Success can also be shared, or attributed to another. In many situations you wouldn't be successful without the help of someone else. But even in acknowledging others' success, you can feel successful. You can succeed in making other people feel very good about themselves.

Each and every thing you do on a daily basis, all of your individual efforts, can generate success on some level. If you look at life on a small scale and notice the abilities that you have grown to take for granted, you will find a myriad of things you accomplish successfully: getting dressed and hitting all the right button holes, driving to work and avoiding all the rough spots in the road, eating lunch without spilling on your new shirt, or simply sharing a smile and brightening someone's day—you see what I mean. Look for success in all the little things you do, in the daily achievements. Feel the elation of successfully being you, a task that no one else on the planet will ever accomplish as well as you.

Life isn't a race to be the best,
it's a challenge to be who you are.
As long as you believe in yourself,
you'll be a shining star.
It's not about what you'll eventually be,
or what you want to do,
it's about being able to take the chance
at being happy being you.

From start to finish in all that you do,
set your own steady pace.
There is no trophy at the end of life,
just the smile that's on your face.

Maybe you'll try to find the niche
that suits you to a T,
or maybe you will go through life
just happy to simply be.
Whatever path you choose to walk
or perhaps the path you fly,
look forward to all the challenges
and the choices you'll have to try.

It doesn't matter who you are,
or what you think you should know:
when you find something you love to do
you're only going to grow.

Despite all you've heard about what you "should" do,
no one can tell you how best to be you.

As you walk your path and draw each breath,
feel glad to be on your way.
Wherever it is you're supposed to go,
just be you and enjoy your day.

Set your sights on what you can do,

not on what you've done.

Know you can instead of think you should,

and you're going to have some fun.

Life won't always be what you expect,
in fact sometimes it's a chore;
to give success a chance to knock,
you may have to build your own door.

Life is more than what you make it,
it's how you enjoy it too;
it won't always be the way you want,
but it can still be right for you.

Don't wait for life to happen, or it will pass you by,
you'll never know how well you can do until you give it a try.

The difference between a want and a need
is all in the effort that first must precede.

Success comes easy when you give it your best,
and important lessons you'll learn:
it's not always about the results at the end,
but also the respect that you earn.

It's not really a secret, this thing we call life:
if you want honey on toast you first need a knife.
Don't rush the sequence that's destined to be;
your life will unfold as it's meant to, you'll see.

Patience

Wait a minute, hold on, relax, be patient. Have you heard this before? Do you find yourself at times unable to wait for a result, or an ending? Where does patience come from—the mind or the soul? Or both? Patience is a virtue. It can be a gift but might also be considered a curse in a fast-paced, hurry-up environment. Some see too much patience as inability to get things done, but having patience simply means being comfortable in the knowledge that a situation will be resolved without undue stress.

I don't know of anyone who has purchased it in a store or found it under a rock while hiking in the woods. Patience, however, can be developed. It can be practiced and over time brought to a workable level. For example, the impatient drivers honking and shaking their fists at the world could, with practice, become tolerant of things on the road out of their control. I am sure there are those out there who would argue, but be patient with me as I am expressing only my thoughts, and I am in no hurry to convince people to be that which they are not. I am simply trying to open the door to the possibility of seeking balance in situations that normally would be stressful.

Recognize each breath. Each one you take completes another moment in time. After several deep breaths, you may no longer be in a hurry, things may no longer be as important as they were a moment ago. You may realize that purely because of distraction, you forgot what it was that you were thinking, and you thought about your breathing instead. This is one path to patience, to accepting things as they are and being happy with things as they unfold. Just like breathing, you can't rush it. Just let it be so it comes naturally.

Don't hold your breath. If relaxing is hard for you right now, be patient. It will come. Breathe through the moments that last the longest, and cherish the ones that pass quickly, because in those moments, I'll bet you were smiling.

Breathe in calm air for a second or two,
and change your perspective to a new point of view.

Take the time to notice things
that happen every day,
and the subtleness of changes made
in a myriad of ways.
Life is always going to happen
whether you see it or not,
but it really helps to calm your soul
if you enjoy the life you've got.

What part of life do you think you are missing?
A goal you have made or dream you are wishing?
Don't focus on things that have yet to be,
but more on the beauty of things you can see:
the life that surrounds you, the smells and the sounds.
Live in the moment with both feet on the ground.

Flowers can grow through granite,
and water can cut through shale,
so learn to see the beauty in things
and that patience will often prevail.

Don't rush through your life, take your time and enjoy it;
we all have calm balance once we learn to employ it.

Life is fleeting when you want it to last,
and tends to drag on when you're waiting,
but either way it's your life to enjoy,
be it tedious or elating.

When you find a path to amble on,
and choose to greet your fate,
things will happen in their own time,
quite often worth the wait.

I'm sure there are times when you wish for next week,
and would be there if you could.
But live for the moment—the one that you're in—
life will unfold as it should.

Remember each moment is precious,
and life passes quickly they say;
so enjoy being you for your whole life
and relax along the way.

There's no way of knowing what the next moment will bring,
but often we wait for some unknown thing.
Let go if you can, and set yourself free:
at least once every day forget time and just be.

Rest

Each day, you have a limited amount of useable energy. This energy doesn't have to be physical—it can be emotional as well. Many of us draw an imaginary line when we know we have had enough. Now that you are thinking about it, you might be smiling in agreement: you have felt this way, you know what this means, and yet, you can't recall drawing this line the last time you were on vacation, or the last time you were doing something that you enjoyed. You hiked to the very top, you rode the entire way, or you did everything you needed to do because you were enjoying doing it. No stress, no lines drawn, no limits reached.

Do you see the pattern evolving? You need to work, work causes stress, stress tires you out, and limits are reached. And it's not just work—if you are doing anything that you don't enjoy, you'll reach those limits quicker. How can this be helped? What if you were to stop what you were doing, if even for a moment, just to breathe, or perhaps to close your eyes and be somewhere that you enjoy. Sometimes simply thinking of things that make you happy can revive you enough to stretch that limit a little further, to make the task a little less challenging. It doesn't take much to revive a person, to refresh a smile and recharge the batteries, so to speak.

I am not sure why our work days are centered around an eight-hour span. Perhaps because eight hours is easy to quarter. With this in mind, every two hours, you should stop what you are doing, stand up, and breathe. For the sake of your health and your happiness, you need to treat yourself with kindness and respect your abilities. You need to take a break as often as required. You need to breathe and to appreciate life for what it is: yours. You only have one chance to live this life in a way that makes you happy. Practice quiet time, relaxing time, happy time, and most important, YOU time.

Balance the work with the rest, the fun with the mundane, and because you are good at what you do, make it fun to do. Why not live a little?

The time that it takes for just a breath
is the time you need to unwind,
and two breaths away is some well-needed peace,
which is very important you'll find.
It's easy to forget how to breathe in calm air,
and we adapt to not even trying,
but then over time we get buried in stress,
and our laughter turns into crying.

There are different ways to reach your calm,
it doesn't matter how.
For some it will take a little while,
for others it will happen now.
The point here is to understand the need
to process all you've viewed,
or before you know it, it's going to happen—
you're going to come unglued.

A moment is captured to spend in reflection,
and the beauty of life becomes real,
as the sun slowly settles behind the horizon,
creating colors we actually feel.
It takes moments like these to help us relax
after a day of doing and being.
We are gently reminded to appreciate life
and find balance in what we are seeing.

How much of life do we miss each day
in a race we'll never win?
How often do you think you're really ahead
when in fact you have yet to begin?
Take some time to relax today,
completely for your own sake.
If just for a moment, put on a smile
and feel the difference that it makes.

Empty your mind and clear your thoughts,
    let a dream take over now;
    just for a moment in your long day,
    you need a break somehow.
You know the spot where you go to think
    and nothing can get in,
no noise, no stress, no troubled thoughts,
    it's where the dream begins.

Your worries will get worse each day
if you can't let go of the stress,
so it's time to be happy being yourself,
and believe that you're doing your best.

Is there anything nicer than to sit with a friend
and watch the world go by?
To forget all your troubles and just rest for a while
and watch the clouds in the sky?
By taking a moment to appreciate life,
you'll find lots of company too;
the world is full of wonderful souls
who will share your smile with you.

Join in the fun by watching the race—
you don't always have to compete;
dream for a moment of where you could be
from the comfort of your seat.
Learn from the others who have run full tilt
and burned out way too fast,
that as long as you're having fun being you,
there's no such thing as last.

Frustration looms in all of us
in a different kind of way,
with the clicks of buttons and flashing screens
now printing what we say.
Reward your senses with real 3D,
just have a walk outside;
smell a flower, breathe the air,
and enjoy nature with every stride.

No matter the weather or the time of day, it's not your job to stew;
right now it's more important to just do what's right for you.

Is there a moment for you in your lifelong quest
to sit down and breathe and have a well-deserved rest?

It doesn't matter where you go in the world,
peaceful is a state of mind:
if you simply believe that you are relaxed,
then peace you will soon find.

In the time that passed while reading these words,

you've taken in fresh relaxed air.

Now start your day with the stress pushed away,

and enjoy the calm smile you share.

Gratitude

Are you grateful for being you? Do you ever look at yourself in the mirror and think that there is no one else you would rather be? You should, because you are the best you there has even been. Is it gratitude if you pat yourself on the back for doing a good job? Of course it is, and you deserve it. Gratitude will not always flow easily. In fact, at times you will really feel you are due some gratitude for something you have done, or completed for others, and it will not come. But if it should happen that you don't receive gratitude from others, you simply need to be grateful that you enjoy being you.

You know the old saying about the grass always being greener on the other side of the fence? Who was it, do you suppose, who came up with that, and why are we so quick to quote that phrase every chance we get? Could it be that we are not giving ourselves the gratitude we deserve for everything we have accomplished, or for everything we already have in our yards? And what if there comes a time in your life when grass just doesn't fit your life? What if you prefer stonework or wildflowers? Then you will no longer compare your yard to those that have grass. In the end, it is enough that you are who you are, and want what you have.

Each and every day can contain something to be grateful for: family, friends, food on the table, a job to go to and a way to get there—or perhaps just the fact that the morning came, the sun rose, and you have another day to be grateful to be alive. It is your responsibility, you know, to be happy with who you are, to be grateful for what you have. And in turn, it is your choice to share your gratitude, and to recognize the things that others have, or don't have, for that matter. What you have may seem better to someone else only because you have it. Remember, "One man's junk is another man's treasure." Be grateful for the grass and the fence.

Look past the wants and fulfill the needs first, then be grateful you have the day to share your smiles with the world. Show your gratitude for being alive by being happy just to be.

Be thankful today for all that you have,
and for the fact that you are you,
be thankful for the beauty of living,
and for your friends and family too.
Be thankful today for all that you have
and for all that you can share,
be thankful for every breath you take
and for that smile that shows you care.

I say to you if you're feeling blue
you should find a happy thought.
All it takes is a moment or two
to remember what you've got.

Sometimes we take what we have for granted
and forget that life is a gift.
We need to remember to appreciate living,
and smile to give us a lift.

Don't count the days until you can,
instead live in the minute.
Though your life has twists and turns,
be happy that you're in it.

Living is full of moments,
individually there are a lot,
and yet we never seem to have the time
to be thankful for what we've got.
Take a moment whenever you can
to be grateful for who you are,
and enjoy the things you already have
before you wish upon that star.

They say the grass is always greener
on the other side of the fence,
but is the color of grass a reason for you
to always be so tense?
Let it go, it's only grass,
it has no effect on you,
instead you should be more concerned
with what it is you do.
There's always someone out there
who is looking in your yard,
so be thankful for the things you've earned—
they came from working hard.

Life should never be measured by
the cost behind some thing;
it should be enjoyed instead
for the smiles that a thing may bring.

In case you need a little review
from a page in the book of living:
life is a gift that we get each day,
and thanks is something for giving.

Don't wait for occasions to appreciate things,
you should be thankful every minute,
because there isn't a day that goes by
without something special that's in it.

Thank you my friends for all your support,

your kindness and your light.

If you weren't here to read my words,

I would have no reason to write.

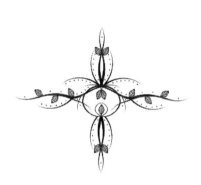

Acknowledgments

I would like to thank the people in my life who have been there to help me along this new and uncharted path on which I walk.

Rachel Small – Editor, Faultless Finish Editing
Carrie Mumford – Proofreader
Jessee Wise – Illustrator
Fiona Raven – Designer

And to the souls in my life who have given me strength, support and inspiration, this adventure would not have happened without you all. Special thanks to all those who share my path, my life and my smiles.

About the Author

Robert (BawB) Chomany is the author of the BawB's Raven Feathers series, pure and simple inspirational books. He was born in Calgary, Alberta, with a clear view of the mountains to the west. These mountains eventually drew Bob in, and he spent many years living in the company of nature, exploring his spiritual side.

Bob pursues his many interests with passion. You are just as likely to find him twisting a wrench, or riding his motorcycle, as you are to find him holding a pen, writing.

Bob still lives in Calgary, where he finds happiness by simply living with a smile and sharing his words of wisdom with others.

Made in the USA
Charleston, SC
20 February 2017